FUZZWIPPERS
PLAY FAIR

MARILYNN HALAS

Illustrated by Jeremy Provost

4 sunflowers
media

A 4 Sunflowers Media FUZZWIPPER Picture Book

Hello! I'm a Fuzzwipper and that's me, Fuzzy, on the swing. That's also me coming down the slide with my friend George. We love to play together at the playground.

We have a lot of fun on swings, climbing the jungle gym and going on the merry-go-round, but our absolute favorite is the slide.

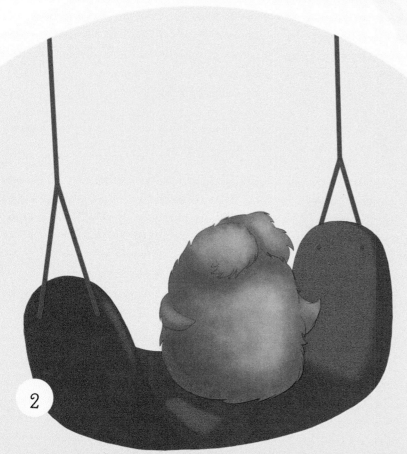

There is nothing like feeling the wind in my fuzz
as we sail down the twists and turns.

Most of the time the slide is our first stop. But sometimes we have to wait because someone else is on it.

The good thing is we don't mind waiting.
Taking turns is part of the fun.

A few days ago George and I went to the playground and we met some new friends. We all climbed the jungle gym and then we went over to the swings.

Everything was great...
until we decided to go to the slide.

Everyone wanted to go down the slide at the same time. It was a little crazy at the bottom of the ladder.

George and I knew right away that we would need to do some talking and some listening so that everyone could have some fun.

"Can we all just take a break and figure this out?"
George asked.

Our friends started to relax and let go of the ladder.
They wanted to know what we had to say.

The next thing we did was smile and remind everyone that we were all on the same side. "I know it can be hard to wait sometimes," George began. "But if we take turns we will get to go down the slide faster than if we keep arguing with each other down here."

I was so proud of my Fuzzwipper friend.

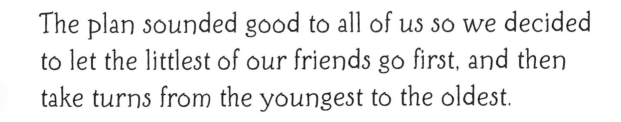

The plan sounded good to all of us so we decided to let the littlest of our friends go first, and then take turns from the youngest to the oldest.

We wanted to show the younger ones that taking turns was always a good way to play fair. That way, everyone can have fun and no one feels left out.

We had more fun at the playground than ever before.

Learning to play fair on the slide meant that we could play fair no matter what we were doing. It felt so good to know what to do and to know we had solved our problem.

That night in George's room, while fireflies danced outside the window, we were happy, but I had a problem. We Fuzzwippers have a very important message to share. How could I tell everyone myself? George had a great idea: could my Fuzzwipper family help?

When we went back to the playground, all of our new friends were there, but they weren't alone anymore. My whole Fuzzwipper family joined us, and everyone became a very special Fuzzwipper friend.

As night came, the sky was filled with the light of fireflies that my Fuzzwipper family had asked to help us spread our very special message: *You are loved, no matter what.*